Divorce
to
Wholeness

Sharon Kay Ball
Paige Henderson

The Freedom Series
Created by Michelle Borquez

AspirePress

Torrance, California

Divorce to Wholeness

© Copyright 2013 God Crazy/Bella Publishing
Aspire Press, a division of Rose Publishing, Inc.
4733 Torrance Blvd., #259
Torrance, California 90503 USA

www.aspirepress.com
Register your book at www.aspirepress.com/register
Get inspiration via email, sign up at www.aspirepress.com

The views and opinions expressed in this book are those of the authors and do not necessarily express the views of Aspire Press, nor is this book intended to be a substitute for mental health treatment or professional counseling.

Scripture taken from the New American Standard Bible, © Copyright 1960, 1962, 1963, 1968, 1971, 1972, 1973, 1975, 1977, 1995 by The Lockman Foundation. Used by permission.

Printed in the United States.

Contents

The Authors

Sharon Kay Ball, licensed professional counselor, is an expert in divorce adjustment, having counseled many women and children in these circumstances. When the trauma of betrayal and infidelity rocked her own world, Sharon's own divorce resulted in newfound ability to blend knowledge with personal experience of divorce to help guide others through their own journeys.

Paige Henderson is sought after nationally and internationally as a speaker who loves unlocking the passion in the hearts of women. Paige and her husband, Richard, founded Fellowship of the Sword Ministries [www.fellowshipofthesword.com].

Chapter 1

Sharon's Story

By Sharon Kay Ball

I always believed life was kind of like the ocean, and I was a surfer. All I had to do was pick the right wave, stay balanced, and I would experience the ride of my life, all the while heading toward a beautiful destination. What I chose to ignore was the fact that storms can come without warning over the ocean, and lurking beneath the beautiful blue-green surface are sharks, stingrays, poisonous jellyfish, and other dangers that want to take you down.

I grew up determined to be a good girl. If I did everything right, that was like catching the right wave. As long as I didn't rock my surfboard, I'd stay on top of life's waves. My life would be smooth surfing, and anything dangerous would stay far beneath me. Skies would stay blue and filled only with puffy, marshmallow-white clouds, and I would glide straight into my happily ever after. Sound a bit naive? Maybe to some, but to me this was reality. This was my dream, to have the "happily ever after." It's what we all strive for.

I was a rule-follower and a goal-setter.

What I didn't know is that the picturesque ocean I had spent so long learning to stay atop would try to overtake me and eventually leave me on the shore of hopelessness when I found myself, as a thirty-something, in the midst of the greatest storm I had ever encountered. By this point in my life, I was professionally counseling others whose lives had gone topsy-turvy. Now I found myself in desperate need of the very hand of hope and healing I was used to offering.

My life's dream, like many other girls, was to get married, have children, and maintain a career. Pretty normal, right? I was an American woman. I was taught that I could have it all. At an early age, I began to believe that if I just followed the rules, kept on being good, and did things the right way, I would get what I wanted. I was a rule-follower and a goal-setter.

Goal No. 1: Marry Mr. Right.

Goal No. 2: Have three beautiful children.

Goal No. 3: Set up a thriving psychotherapy practice.

My focus on being good and following the rules worked at first. I received praise for being good, I liked the success that came with hard work, and I easily adapted to others' expectations. I began to define myself by my dreams and by how other people saw me, instead of seeking the will of my heavenly Father and desiring his approval of me.

On the surface everything was going just fine. Goal No. 1: Check. Goals 2 and 3: Check and double-check.

But after sixteen years of trying everything in my power to hold it together, my marriage capsized. When there had been betrayal in the past, I had patched it up, sucked it up, and gone on with our lives. Not just for me, but for our children. My life could not fall apart. It would destroy everything I had ever believed in and known to be true. But it did. My marriage washed completely away. The storm had come, and now I felt as if I would drown in my tears and pain.

My life could not fall apart. It would destroy everything I had ever believed in.

We had almost divorced once before when I was pregnant with our third child, but I rode the wave of focusing on my marriage at all costs. I was teetering, but I was determined. I took a year off from work, he quit touring, and I kept riding the wave. Betrayal was all around me. I had to fight not to become resentful and bitter, but I knew more than anything that I had to press on … for me, for the kids, for our families, and God.

I clung to my board even when the waves became tsunami-sized. The betrayal and lies continued, but I could not, would not, give up my dream. What would other people think? Good girls, Christians, overachievers like me did not get divorced. I was a psychotherapist for goodness' sake. Couldn't I get to the bottom of the issues in my own marriage and fix them? The weight of the waves crashing over me began to wear me down. I grew weary by the day. Can you relate? If you have experienced divorce, I am sure you can.

As weak as I was, I continued to grasp and cling

to any ounce of hope I could find, only to feel as if my head was being pushed under the water over and over again. Papers in hand, attorneys present, I no longer could live in denial. This was my life. This was real. It was happening to me and there was absolutely nothing I could do. My children's tears, the hard reality of my new life as a single mother, quickly jolted me out of my dreams and made me realize that life as I knew it for sixteen years was over. No more happily ever after. I thought in that moment I had lost it all: my marriage, my children's innocence, my chance for love. All gone. All washed up.

God never promised us a perfect life. What he did promise me was that he would never leave me nor would he ever forsake me, even in my darkest moments, my tsunami storms. This was the hope I had to hang on to. The deep blue ocean I had once only known from afar, thinking that avoiding its predators—the sharks, the poisonous jellyfish—would keep me safe and happy, was now the very thing God was using to teach me. He taught me that in the depths of the ocean, in the midst of the pain and trials, the things life brings to destroy us are the very things he uses to reveal his bountiful love for us. No longer would I fear the ocean and its darkness. Instead I have allowed it to wash over me, cleanse me of my own sin, my own prideful nature, and show me that my value is not based on my performance, but it is rooted in Christ's deep love and acceptance of me just as I am.

> When my despair could go no deeper, I surrendered.

When my despair could go no deeper, I surrendered. I could not make my marriage work. I could not fix the heartache my children were going through. I had to stop fighting the waves and allow them to wash over me. When I finally did, I was weak and shaken to the core, but in my weakness God became strong. My trust had to be in him. I learned to entrust my future to him. I didn't understand it. I couldn't fix it. I didn't feel it was deserved, and yet I have entrusted the outcome of my life completely to him— and this is not a one-time act of surrender, but a daily revelation.

> I slowly learned to accept that... my value is not measured by my failures or wounds.

It wasn't instant or easy. As I grieved over the next couple of years, God slowly showed me how to be kind and gentle to myself. I grieved deeply over my shattered dreams, yet he began to reveal the high cost my soul had paid for clinging to what I desired instead of asking my Savior what his plans were for me. I wanted the special man, kids, and career; and maybe God wanted that for me too, but not in my own strength. Not on my terms. Not when I based my success and self-worth on the approval of everyone but him.

Tenderly, Jesus showed me that I had limits and wounds. My wounds needed to be tended to, but accepting that I was wounded was hard. I saw wounds as failure, and failure deserves punishment. Over time, God taught me through his Word, prayer, and wise counsel how to grieve my losses without taking them out on myself. I slowly learned to accept that bad things do happen to good people and my value is not measured by my failures or wounds.

It's amazing how you can teach something, help other people find those answers, and yet until you experience the depths of trials yourself, you are unable to truly understand what it means to press through to the victory. I am not a victim. I could not control the choices of someone else. I did not want a divorce nor did I want to ever be a single mother. This was not God's will, but God does not force his will on others. He is a gentleman and allows people to make choices. I just never realized someone's choices could impact my life so deeply that it would change it forever.

I remember my spiritual counselor asking me to close my eyes and tell her where I pictured Jesus. Was he in

> Through this surrender, I could finally see that Jesus had not abandoned me.

the room with me or outside the door? Weeping, I responded that I saw Jesus on a boat in the ocean, leaving me as I sat on the beach. That was where I saw Jesus in my life. I felt completely abandoned and alone. This wasn't fair. I had tried to do everything "right." How could he let it all go wrong? In my heart, Jesus had bailed on me. He left me in my darkest hours. He left me because my "right" wasn't good enough for him. I wasn't good enough for him.

What I longed for deep in my soul was Jesus to have rescued me from the tsunami. Where was he in the tsunami? Why didn't he save me? I longed for Jesus to hold me and whisper to me, "You are loved and you are beautiful to me no matter what storms you have had to battle through." I didn't feel lovable. I didn't feel I deserved to be loved. Most of all, I didn't want Jesus to abandon me like my husband had.

God's journey of grief for me started out as my enemy but grew to be my closest friend. Grief took me to dark places I feared, but then God used grief to show me he was strong enough to handle it. Grief stripped me of all my "right" ways of doing life so I could learn to let him do it his way.

Through this surrender, I could finally see that Jesus had not abandoned me. He was with me in the waves, watching over me; he was the gentleman giving me space to come to the end of myself. During many dark nights, he watched over me. When I called to him, he would quickly come ashore and join me on the desolate beach.

"You are loved, you are beautiful, you are wanted," he told me again and again. He told me to rest in him. He called me his "good and faithful daughter." Jesus knew exactly what I needed to hear.

Eventually, my wounds began to heal, and the healing continues. Yes, they left scars, but those scars are good reminders that I don't ever want to surf under my own strength again, and eventually even scars fade. They are also evidence of the newfound strength I have in him. The strength to be weak, the strength to give up everything so I can have it all, the strength to lose my own grip on life so I could gain it, and most of all the strength to not resist the waves in life that appear to overtake me, because they won't, not with him carrying me through.

My divorce left me abandoned and alone on the beach of desolation, but Jesus would never leave me there. Once I looked to him, he led me back down to the water's edge. And as long as I stepped out humbly and let him lead the way, this time I would walk on waves of living water. My steps were tentative. It's tough to be humble, but I learned to reach out and ask close friends and my church for help when I needed groceries. I learned to reach out to my dad at three o'clock in the morning and be vulnerable enough to just weep over the phone, sometimes unable to articulate anything. In my weakness, God was made strong in me.

> When I let go of my dreams, I experienced a reawakening of my soul.

When I let go of my dreams, I experienced a reawakening of my soul. I even became grateful for those tsunami-size waves (although truthfully I'd prefer not to be battered by them again) that tried to take me down to the depths. That's the paradox of the gospel, isn't it? When we come to the end of ourselves, when we are washed up on the dry beach of desolation, he is always right there, ready to comfort, ready to heal, ready to stretch out his mighty hand and pull you gently back out to sea.

Chapter 2

Bible Study

by Paige Henderson

Let Me Pour Us a Cup o' Truth

What do you do when bad things interrupt what seems to be a pretty okay life? What do you do when the last thing you want to happen, happens?

A woman was interviewed in the aftermath of a tornado that tore through her little town. She likely was saved by the storm shelter she had in the backyard. When asked to describe the event, she said that when she ran into the storm cellar, her house was there. But when she came out, it was gone! Just a slab remained.

She went in search of what she could find, and then she would see about starting over.

Can you relate this woman's description of the tornado's destruction to what you see as you look around at the aftermath of divorce? A marriage was there, and then it wasn't. And now there is the debris.

From Sharon's Story

"God never promised us a perfect life."

This study is about resetting and recovering some truths and issues that may have been knocked around and blown around by this season of divorce. God is still good and you are still loved by him. He is working in and through these hard and sometimes harsh circumstances to bring you to a place of wholeness and completeness in him.

When "Fair" and "Perfect" Crumble

Did you read Sharon's story feeling like you were watching another fairy tale dashed to the ground in pieces? Our world says that good people should have good lives. That's what feels "fair" to us. If we follow the rules, we get a wonderful life in return. But it doesn't always work out that way.

We have to be very careful to separate biblical truth from cultural values. God didn't promise us a perfect life or a fair one. However, he does intend to make you perfect to live your life. So first we'll look at "fair" and then we'll take care of "perfect."

Read Matthew 5:38 and write it below. This is part of Jesus' teaching in his Sermon on the Mount.

_____

_____

_____

_____

_____

_____

That verse sounds "fair," doesn't it? But Jesus came to shift the paradigm of understanding who God is, not just what he does or what he allows to happen. Jesus came to unlock the heart and expose behavior in a society that was all about behavior and "fair." He came to complete the picture of God and to fully manifest what God meant when he created the world and poured himself into it. (Those are not the only reasons he came, but they're good for what we're doing here!)

Notice how the next verse (v. 39) begins: "But I say to you…" The word "but" indicates that something is now different from what came previously. Jesus is setting up a parallel between what the Old Testament Law says and what he says to complete the full picture—which is what he just stated a couple of verses up in Matthew 5:17.

Now read Matthew 5:39–42. Fill in the rest of these statements:

If someone slaps you, _____

_____

_____

_____

If someone sues you and takes the shirt off your back, _____

_____

_____

_____

If someone makes you walk a mile, _____

_____

_____

Now **read Matthew 5:43** and write it below.

_____

_____

_____

_____

_____

Sounds "fair" again, doesn't it? However there's another "but" in the very next verse. Go on and **read verses 44–47** and answer the questions that correspond to them.

About verse 44:

Who do you love?

_____

_____

_____

_____

Who do you pray for?

_____

_____

_____

_____

About verse 45:

What is the purpose of loving and praying?

_____

_____

_____

_____

Who gets sunshine in their lives?

_____

_____

_____

_____

Who gets rain in their lives?

_____

_____

_____

_____

Thought Question: Is the blessing of a good marriage or the curse of a broken one God's way of "repaying" you for what you've done in your past—good or bad?

About verses 46 and 47:

What do these two verses say about life being easy or perfect? (You may want to read these two verses in different versions of the Bible if you have them.)

_____

_____

_____

_____

_____

Now **read verse 48** and write it below.

_____

_____

_____

_____

_____

Thought Question: The word "therefore" ties a section of thought together into a conclusion. The section of thought here is from verse 38 to verse 48. What is the Lord saying to you right now as it applies to your experience with divorce?

What does the idea of being "perfect" make you think of? Is it achievable or not? Is it an attractive thought for you, like you really want that in your life?

Consider the definition of the word "perfect": complete, of full age or growth. The root of the word "perfect" is the Greek word *telos* which means "to set out for a definite point or goal."

What is "perfect" to you? Is it hitting the target every time? Scoring 100 out of 100 on every quiz? Having flawless skin and glossy hair, and never being wrong in your decisions or choices? This kind of perfect is man-centered ("Look at what I can do!") and competitive ("See me be better than you!"). Jesus' call to perfect is God-centered and only requires your cooperation with his work in your life to be attained by everybody who seeks it!

I want to be complete and full grown. I'm ready to set out for a definite point or goal and to stop sitting and waiting for "perfect" to fall on me. How about you? Are you ready to take off that last-season, wrong-color-palette coat of life-smothering perfection? Celebrate completeness and the difficulties and mistakes and "unfortunates" that are needed to get us there!

God is much more interested in what you do with your circumstances and what you become as a result of your circumstances than he is about your circumstances themselves. But that doesn't mean that he doesn't care. Here's what the apostle Peter has to say about that:

"Therefore humble yourselves under the mighty hand of God, that he may exalt you at the proper time, casting all your anxiety on him, because he cares for you."

—1 Peter 5:6–7

Let's go through this, idea by idea:

Humble yourselves... This is an act of bowing your heart more than it is bowing your body. We can prostrate ourselves before God and not intend full submission. This phrase indicates an act of the will. Humility isn't taken from you; you give it.

...under the mighty hand of God... The idea of the "hand" actually includes everything from the shoulder down the whole arm, including the hand. The root of the word is a storm rivulet, a hollow, or chasm through which storm water flows. Consider God's whole arm as a conduit of blessing and victory, flowing down and out his fingertips for you. This is not a hand of oppression; it's a channel of resources. What he has for you is mighty, powerful, and potent for what your needs are.

…exalt you at the proper time… Exalt is not lavishing with honors and gifts, but rather simply lifting up into the air. At the right time, the time that is most fitting for your good and his glory, he will lift you up! A change of perspective comes when you are lifted out of where you are and allowed to see where you're going.

…casting all your anxiety on him… To cast is to fling from one object onto another. You are flinging onto God every care and worry and anxiety—those things that divide your focus and distract your thoughts from the presence and power of God. Take those things and fling them on him. They'll stick. He can take them all!

...because he cares for you. What you are going through matters. It matters to him. He's not just interested, he's concerned, and his invitation to cast those anxieties onto him is based on the fact that all those worries really matter.

Let's finish up this "becoming perfect" idea with **James 1:2–4**. To make this more personal, substitute your name for the word "brethren" or "brothers and sisters" in verse 2.

How are you encouraged to face trials?

_____

_____

_____

What does "tested faith" produce?

_____

_____

_____

_____

_____

What is the result of endurance?

_____

_____

_____

_____

There's that "perfect" word again! Perhaps the Bible version you're using translates the word as "fully mature" or "fully developed," but it's still the same word for "perfect" used in Matthew 5:48. Does that surprise you? Well, this is a Bible study designed to make a point and heal your heart. God is after completeness and wholeness in you.

A Thought to Sip On

Good things happen to bad people and bad things happen to good people. Divorce doesn't happen because you didn't have your Quiet Time or because you got drunk at a party in high school and lied to your parents, or because you stole a pack of gum from the convenience store when you were six. God isn't running a swap meet: "You give me your time every morning, and I'll give you a perfect marriage."

The point that Jesus was making, and then Peter and James after him, is that your life, your heart, your whole being is at stake here, not just your pretty circumstances. Jesus didn't die for your circumstances—which includes your marriage. He died for you.

Reflect: Write your thoughts below. Is there anything wrong with having dreams for your life? Why? How about plans, are they good to make? Why?

_____

_____

_____

_____

_____

_____

_____

_____

_____

_____

_____

When You Feel Like You're Losing It

Read Romans 8:35–39.

What is the first word of verse 35?

_____

_____

_____

_____

It's not "what," it's "who." Who shall separate us? Hmm. I wonder where the apostle Paul is going with this? Is there a difference between a "who" and a "what"? I know it's basic, but basic understanding is where deep revelation comes from!

From Sharon's Story

"I thought ... I had lost it all."

Let's move on to the list that the apostle Paul offers in verse 35. There are seven potential separators mentioned. List them in the space below. This is not an exhaustive list; it's just a partial one!

1. _____

2. _____

3. _____

4. _____

5. _____

6. _____

7. _____

Looks like a big list of "what's" to me! But the Lord is speaking something deeper to you. Behind all those "what's" is a "who." Think about it: none of those things happen without affecting a whole lot of "who's," right? There's a "who" that started it, did it, made it, and a "who" that got stuck with it, paid for it, had to overcome it. Blame bubbles to the surface over who started it, who deserved it, who caused it. Or, there were two "who's" that brought it to each other.

There are a number of ways that we hurt each other, and then because of the hurt, we feel separated from God. It seems that we use our hurt more to drive a wedge in our relationship with the Lord, rather than using that hurt as a wrapping to bind our hearts to his.

Allow me to give some deeper definitions to the list of words that Paul gives in verse 35. Consider each one as it affects you right now.

"Who will separate us from the love of Christ? Will tribulation, or distress, or persecution, or famine, or nakedness, or peril, or sword?".

—Romans 8:35

Tribulation is pressure. The word involves a crowd or throng, crushing and pressing you. Have you felt like that in your divorce? "What are people going to think?" "I'm letting everybody down." The pressure—tribulation—comes from the outside and squeezes you. This can't separate you from the love of Christ.

Distress means "narrowness of room." In our vernacular, we would say that the walls are closing in. "What am I going to do?" "I can't stop this from happening." You might feel like you've lost control; like all the circumstances of your divorce have created a down chute and you're at the mercy of gravity. This pressure comes from the inside. It's the pressure you put on yourself, but it cannot separate you from the love of Christ.

Persecution means hot, hostile pursuit. It's the idea of being chased, particularly by enemies. You are being tracked, out in the open with no place in sight to hide. "There's nowhere to hide." "I have no safe place!" "Where can I go?" Their persecution cannot separate you from the love of Christ.

Famine is exactly what it sounds like. This is pure, nothing-fancy hunger, a deep want of food. But let's consider the hunger of your heart for a moment. Are you walking in a deep, echoing emptiness? "This is taking all my strength." "I have nothing left to give." This hunger in your heart and soul cannot separate you from the love of Christ.

Nakedness is also what it seems to be: literal nudity. But consider again your heart. Has your divorce stripped you of what you used to create your image? There's nothing left to cover yourself and in all the proceedings and documents you might feel very alone. "I feel exposed and vulnerable." "The things on the outside that protected me are gone." "Everyone knows and all eyes are on me." The severity of this aloneness cannot separate you from the love of Christ.

Peril is danger. The word intimates that once you were in safety and then something happened, by your choice or by someone else's actions, to plunge you into danger. There has been a movement, a shift, and it has put you in a battle zone. You are in "fight or flight" mode all the time. "I don't feel safe." "Something terrible is going to happen any minute." Even here, you cannot be separated from the love of Christ.

Sword is simply a weapon of war. But when the sword comes out, there is no peace. It's this lack of peace that seems to be the first to greet you in the morning and the last thing on your mind when you lay down to sleep. "I have no peace." "Will there ever be a peaceful moment, a peaceful thought again?" "When will I enjoy my life, myself, again?" Peacelessness cannot separate you from the love of Christ.

Do you feel the power of the Word seeping into your soul? The dissolution of a marriage seems to be something that would perfectly illustrate what Paul was trying to tell us. Signing on the line next to the attorney's sticky note isn't what hurts. What hurts is the deeply personal nature of a broken relationship.

Which of these words have you experienced? Which do you feel like you're right in the middle of? Explain how you see it being "fleshed" out in your current situation.

_____

_____

_____

_____

_____

_____

_____

_____

Divorce to Wholeness

_____

_____

_____

_____

_____

_____

_____

_____

_____

_____

_____

_____

_____

_____

_____

_____

_____

Life: Take it for a Spin!

Read Ecclesiastes chapter 3, verses **1–8**, and then verses **11–12**.

If you've seen the movie *Footloose*, these words in Ecclesiastes are familiar to you! Well at least up to the end of verse 4 ("...a time to dance") because that's all the young man in the movie needed to quote to make his point; then all the kids erupt into maniacal applause and you wouldn't have been able to hear the rest of the verses anyway! So it's good that we're reading them now.

From Sharon's story

"I grieved deeply over my shattered dreams."

What do you see in all these verses? Are these opposites? Are they choices? Or are they complete cycles, marking the starting point and the ending point and returning to the starting point?

I believe they are cycles and at any moment in our lives we are at some point on all of them. Some of you are experiencing the beginning of some of those cycles listed, some of you are at the end and some of you reading this are in the middle. And then there are all the stages in between. If they are cycles, then both halves are necessary, right? Like the first one, the life cycle involves birth and death. You can't have one without the other.

Let's look at verse 4 again: "A time to weep and a time to laugh; A time to mourn and a time to dance."

If these are cycles and not opposites or choices, then what is the natural end of weeping?

_____

_____

_____

_____

_____

_____

What is the natural end of mourning?

_____

_____

_____

_____

_____

If these are natural cycles, then can you skip either the beginning or the end? Like birth and death in the life cycle, neither the beginning nor the end can be skipped. If you excuse yourself from the first word of the cycle, then you will fail to experience the second. If you want to be exempt from the first part, you will also exempt yourself from the second.

We'd love to just not have to weep or mourn. Couldn't you just skip to the end? Just get through this part and move on?

"Chin up!" "Never let 'em see you sweat!" "Everything's OK." "I'll be fine." These are actually blockages—like big orange highway department barricades—that will keep you from getting to Part 2 of the process. Just like a true cycle, it's not complete until both parts have come. Like a CD that can't be read in the player, you will loop and loop and loop and never get to the end.

Weeping and mourning are the first steps to the complete cycle. There is an end to the cycle and it ends on an upswing! To every story there is a beginning, middle, and an end. The story of loss as you walk through this time has a beginning, middle and an end. Make sure that you don't get stuck in the loop of grief. There is laughing and dancing waiting for you. If you've reached that part and you were wondering if it was right to be there, it is. Enjoy!

A Thought to Sip On

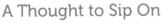 Living things grow and growing things change. Love is living because God is love and he is living. Love is alive. Love is God, and he grows to be bigger than whatever the "next big thing" in your life is. You cannot fathom the depths of his love for you, nor can you imagine anything so insurmountable that he is not bigger still. Here's the really amazing part: He doesn't change as we move closer to him, our perspective changes and we see something new that we've never seen before. When we look to him instead of away from him in times of desperate need, he reveals part of himself that we've never seen before. It is an intimate invitation to believe him.

As you move closer to the Lord at this time in your life, he will show you new things about himself—his character, his love, his provision, his protection. This new revelation is what you are persevering to see! Your endurance will bear the fruit of completing you, perfecting you for the next adventure he has for your life.

The Best Laid Plans...

From Sharon's Story

"When I let go of my dreams, I experienced a reawakening of my soul."

Here's the next topic to talk about: Is there anything wrong with having dreams and making plans?

Was Sharon wrong to have those dreams?

There's a proverb that says, "We can make our plans, but the LORD determines our steps" (Proverbs 16:9 NLT).

Does that sound like you should or shouldn't make plans?

The problem with the dreams we have is that in our minds they've already happened. We've already had dinner parties in the dollhouse of our dreams, complete with the perfect husband

and lots of pretty friends. We've picked out names for the kids and clothes for the husband. We write scripts for our lives and expect God to read his lines and appear on cue.

This issue here is not having dreams and plans, but it's really how much we're attached to them—and whether we'll let God conform them to his will for us. If we clutch them to our chests like a four-year-old protecting her dolly—"Mine!"—then in a way we've made an idol out of them. We hang onto what we know tightly because letting go sometimes means a free-fall into the unknown. Will we hit bottom? Will we stop somewhere along the way? Is there a big blade down there somewhere that will chop us in half if we don't have skills like a movie-screen spy?

In the book of Jeremiah the Lord gives his people instruction on how to live outside the plans that they once had and embrace the place in which they find themselves.

Read Jeremiah 29:4–14.

God's people had been conquered by their enemies and carried off to Babylon far away from their home. They are a defeated people who are being marched into a life of exile. Do you feel like you're in exile because of your divorce? Do you feel exiled from friends? From family? Even from your church? Does it seem like you were whisked away in the night from a place of familiarity to a place of discomfort? That's what exile feels like.

What does God tell the people of Israel to do while in exile in verses 5–7?

_____

_____

_____

_____

_____

_____

Where's the mourning? Where's the self-pity? Where's the contempt for their captors? Where's the desire for revenge? It's not there, is it? God tells his people, in the words of a very old adage, to bloom where they are planted. He wants them to thrive where they are, not just survive. How can they do this? How can you do that when everything seems so foreign and unsynchronized? Could it be that you will be able to flourish, not just maintain, when you recognize that God has given you a strategic instruction to do so?

Picture God gathering all of his people around him like a coach in the middle of a team huddle, giving the strategy to the team: "You're not going to like being where you are, but get in there and live!"

The strategy that God gives them is based on his goodness, his accessibility, and his plan for their restoration.

Read verses 11–13.

Who knows the plans that God has for you?

_____

_____

_____

_____

What is the goal of those plans for you?

_____

_____

_____

_____

What will the plans of God not result in for you?

_____

_____

_____

_____

What will happen when you pray?

_____

_____

_____

_____

What will happen when you look for him?

_____

_____

_____

_____

When your plans fall apart, look to God's plans. You can spend so much time mourning what was lost that you miss the blessing of what God is doing—even if what he's doing looks very much like exile. I don't know what you hear in these verses, but I do not hear an angry voice coming from God as he instructs. I hear love. I hear the voice of a Father who loves his children—and you, his child—giving them hope. Although he may be hard to see right now in what you're going through, he's not hiding. You may not hear him speaking to you—but it's because he's listening to you. He has a good plan focused on your well-being that will restore you to wholeness.

And On Our Left You'll See the Potter's House

From Sharon's Story

"Through this surrender, I could finally see that Jesus had not abandoned me."

One day God took the prophet Jeremiah on a field trip to the local pottery shop to give him a picture of what God's sovereignty looks like. God is like the Potter (which is why I am capitalizing the word like a name) and we are like the clay.

Read Jeremiah 18:1–12.

Verse 4 could easily be discouraging if we don't spend some time there. What happens to the clay that is on the wheel?

_____

_____

_____

_____

_____

Where is the clay when it is "spoiled"? (Some translations say "marred")

_____

_____

_____

_____

_____

Here's the first point: When the clay is spoiled it is in the Potter's hand. I don't know if you've ever watched a pot being "thrown." (You "throw" pottery when you shape it on the spinning wheel—that's your potting vocabulary for the day!) If you have, you know that the potter never takes his hand off that lump of clay. Every movement of the hand of the potter is reflected in the shape of the pot. If the potter takes his hand off the spinning clay, the clay will become a victim of centrifugal force and will immediately become misshapen.

In Jeremiah, the ruining of the pot didn't happen because of the Potter's neglect. It happened while in the Potter's hand. There was a flaw, a weak spot that caused the pot to be unusable at that moment.

Continue in verse 4. What does the Potter do with the clay?

_____

_____

_____

_____

_____

_____

Did you think that the Potter would throw the clay away? He uses that very lump of clay. He doesn't pitch that "bad" clay into the trash and get some more to take its place. He uses the same clay, still moldable and still in his hand to start over and make something else.

Wow! In this process of walking through your divorce, have you felt thrown away? Have you felt defective and unusable? The Potter isn't like that at all. Just like the clay, you are still usable and he likes the essential ingredients of who you are enough to make something else out of you. You are not throw-away-able. (That's not a word, but it's the best one for here and now.) You are re-purpose-able.

Things fall apart. Stuff causes a breakdown in the original plan. Okay. The Potter starts over.

Finish verse 4. What kind of vessel does the Potter make with the clay that he's re-forming?

_____

_____

_____

_____

_____

It pleases him to make something new out of you, not to trash you because you are flawed. There is nothing that can happen to you, the clay, that the Potter can't do something else with. Is it time for a re-formation in your life? Stay for one more revolution of the wheel and see what he's making out of you.

"...for it is God who is at work in you, both to will and to work for His good pleasure."

—Philippians 2:13

You are in the hands of a Master Sculptor. You may not have any idea how he's going to fix you or what he's going to do, but you don't have to. You aren't the expert; he is. He's holding you in his hand, touching you expertly, forming you, pressing you, shaping you. He's rubbing out the flaws that caused the collapse in the first place, strengthening the weak sides so they're not fragile anymore, filling in the faults with his fingers. Simply put, he's molding clay. You might miss the depth of this in the simplicity. Be careful (wink)! The Potter is making a pot. He's not creating the surroundings for the pot. He's just making a pot. The focus of the Potter is not the shaping of circumstances, but the shaping of your soul. You are the project in the hand of the Potter. Life's issues are not on the wheel. His only focus is you. In his hand. On the wheel.

Look at Me! Look at Me!

From Sharon's Story

"During many dark nights, [Jesus] watched over me."

"Watch me!" "Look at me!" "Hey! Hey! "Come see what I can do!" That's the soundtrack on Christmas morning at my house. All the kids want all the adults to see everything they do at every moment they do whatever they are doing. And they'd really like you to take pictures. I think it's delightful—for about an hour. Then I'm worn out. If you have children at all, you've been dragged off the couch away from the last fifteen minutes of some great movie to stand on the front porch and watch a six-year-old not do a cartwheel. And then you clap, "Yay!"

Something in us wants to be seen and it's been there since the very beginning. That desire is in the Bible. Yep!

David asked God to keep him "as the apple of the eye" (Psalm 17:8). Our culture defines the "apple of the eye" as sort of a favorite thing. If someone is the "apple" of another's eye, they are preferred, indulged a little bit, adored. All that is true. But let's go deeper. The apple of the eye is the center of it, the pupil. The pupil betrays the focus. You know whether someone is looking at you or not by watching the pupils. Have you ever tried to talk to someone who kept looking off? Their eyes darted all around and you just knew they were not in any way concentrating on you.

What David is asking the Lord to do is look at him, focus on him, watch him. But not just to observe him like me watching the kids on Christmas morning. When God keeps you as the apple of his eye, his gaze is for your protection and your comfort. David is asking God to really see him, guard him, and protect him.

Read the surrounding verses, **Psalm 17:5–9**.

Do you sense a concern in David? He needs God's protection. Do you? David asks for God's help to keep from slipping. Do you need that help? David needs the assurance that God is watching over him. Do you need that assurance?

In the space below, write down what you need from the Lord at this moment. Then take that to him in prayer. Ask him to keep looking at you, watching over you, and not to take his eyes off of you.

_____

_____

_____

_____

_____

_____

_____

_____

_____

A Thought to Sip On

Before we move on, let's take the Potter revelation back to the verses in 1 Peter we started with. Look again at **1 Peter 5:6–7**. Consider it now in the context of the Potter and clay. Now when you read this verse, what do you think and feel?

_____

_____

_____

_____

How do you humble yourself under the mighty hand of God? Well it probably means that you have to stay on the Potter's wheel. You'll be dizzy, but you'll be complete. His exalting of you will be the day that the old stone pottery wheel slowly grinds to a stop like a merry-go-round out of children and he lifts you gently from your place in the center of his attention. He will raise you up—still in his hand—and announce, "Look what I made!"

At the right time, when this part of your life is complete and you have moved into a new place of usability, the "ruined" days will slip away behind you. And it is my hope for you that you will smile.

Have you reached that spot yet? Do you feel like the spinning has stopped? Are you still firmly attached to a whirling wheel? Reflect for a while in the space below.

_____

_____

_____

Next Cup o' Truth

One of the deepest hurts of divorce is the loss of approval or acceptance, whether real or perceived. You hear the disapproving sighs, see the "what a shame" smirks and endure the "poor girl" pity. Relationships with "couple friends" can be strained and activity in the church slams to a halt. There's a big scarlet "D" stamped on your forehead.

From Sharon's Story

"My value ... is rooted in Christ's deep love and acceptance of me just as I am."

And then there's the failure aspect—that you just couldn't work it out. But that's circumstantial. The greater failure would be that you don't allow God to work through the broken circumstances. He is working in all aspects of your life and in all circumstances—successes and failures—to bring you to completeness and wholeness. He is working out his good plans for you, molding you and shaping you into the woman he has purposed for you to be. Don't miss what he's doing in you and for you; it's all because of his deep love and acceptance of you.

Read Psalm 139.

But before you read it, let me give you a little insight to this psalm, and to all the psalms really. These psalms were not written to be collected in a book for people to read silently and contemplate. They were written as songs intended to be sung out loud. Singing uses the voice. The voice speaks life.

"Death and life are in the power of the tongue and those who love it eat its fruit."

—Proverbs 18:21

So when you read Psalm 139, read it out loud as a declaration of truth. Really feel the personal words: "me" and "my" and "I." This is your story. Declare it over and over as many times as you need to in order to fill up.

Was there a particular verse in this psalm that was a source of comfort for you? Write it below.

_____

_____

_____

_____

_____

_____

Was there a particular verse that was difficult for you to say? Why do you think it was hard?

_____

_____

_____

_____

_____

From Sharon's Story

Trust

"My trust had
to be in God."

Trust. Can you write a definition for it? Try in the space below. After your definition, write three synonyms (words that mean the same thing) and then write an antonym, a word that means the opposite. ("Distrust" or "mistrust" may not be your antonym!)

Definition:_____

_____

_____

_____

_____

_____

Synonyms:

1. _____

2. _____

3. _____

Antonym:_____

_____

_____

_____

_____

_____

There are ten different translations and definitions of the word "trust" in the Bible: six in the Old Testament and four in the New Testament.

Below is a list of the different words for trust in Hebrew and Greek in the Bible. Read through them. Look the verses up in several translations if you want to. Let them settle into your understanding and then move on.

These are the various ideas for "trust" from Hebrew in the Old Testament:

Chasah—To flee (headlong, overrun your feet, run for your life) for protection; to confide in; have hope; make refuge. (Ruth 2:12; Psalm 7:1)

"He will cover you with His pinions, and under His wings you may trust; His faithfulness is a shield and bulwark."
—Psalm 91:4

Batach (Mibtach)—To hurry for refuge; be confident or sure; be bold; careless/carefree; make to hope. (Job 8:14; Psalm 4:5; 40:4; 71:5; 125:1; Proverbs 22:19)

"O my God, in You I trust. Do not let me be ashamed; do not let my enemies exult over me."—Psalm 25:2

Aman—To build up or support; to foster as a parent or nurse; to be firm or faithful; to be permanent or quiet. (Micah 7:5)

"Then they would put their trust in God, and would not forget his deeds, but would keep his commands."—Psalm 78:7 (NIV)

Yachal—To wait; to be patient; hope; be pained; tarry, stay. (Job 13:15)

"My righteousness is near, My salvation had gone forth, and My arms will judge the people. The coastlands will wait for Me, and for My arm they will trust."—Isaiah 51:5

Hayil—To twist or whirl in a circular or spiral manner; to dance; to writhe in pain; to wait, bear, bring forth, calve, grieve, hope, tremble, wait carefully.

"How much less when you say you do not behold Him, the case is before Him, and you must trust Him!"—Job 35:14

Machseh—A shelter.

"But as for me, the nearness of God is my good; I have made the Lord God my refuge, that I may tell of all Your works."
—Psalm 73:28

Now let's jump into the New Testament and the Greek words for "trust."

Elpizo—To expect or confide.

"And again Isaiah says, 'There shall come the root of Jesse, and He who arises to rule over the Gentiles, In Him shall the Gentiles trust.'"—Romans 15:12 (The "root of Jesse" is a reference to Jesus.)

Peitho—To convince to be true or false by argument; to pacify or conciliate (come to an understanding). (Mark 10:24)

"...indeed, we had the sentence of death within ourselves in order that we should not trust in ourselves, but in God who raises the dead..."—2 Corinthians 1:9

Pisteuo—To have faith in, with respect to a person or thing; credit; to entrust one's spiritual well-being to Christ; believe. (Luke 16:11)

"...but just as we have been approved by God to be trusted with the gospel, so we speak, not as pleasing men but God, who examines our hearts."—1 Thessalonians 2:4

Pepoithesis—Reliance; confidence.

"And such trust we have through Christ toward God."—2 Corinthians 3:4

Which definition most closely matched how
you defined "trust" from the start?

_____

_____

_____

_____

_____

Which definition jumps out at you as the kind
of trust you need right now?

_____

_____

_____

Which verse really ministers to and comforts
your heart and mind? Write that verse below
and make it personal. Put your name in it.

Include a reference to your circumstances. If you need to include someone else's name in your writing, go ahead.

_____

_____

_____

_____

_____

_____

_____

A Thought to Sip On

Trust him to be God. Trust him to be all-knowing and all-powerful. But if you trust him to perform for you, you will be disappointed. I don't trust God to do what

I want him to do. I trust him to do what he wants to do.

Trust has to be based on the goodness of God that he declares to be true. When you come to a crisis that tests your belief system, at the root of the test is your trust. In this is the key to your healing: you will not be intimate with someone you don't trust. Your intimacy with the Lord, which is your source of strength and healing, is dependent upon your trust of him.

You can trust him; his eye is on you. His plans for you are great and you haven't been disqualified from them. Being in relationship with Jesus doesn't guarantee immunity to disappointing circumstances. That relationship gives you access to healing and wholeness. Identify the loss as loss and grieve what's gone. Then embrace that his gift to you is laughter and dancing. Life will move you toward completeness.

The Lord says, "I have put before you life and death, the blessing and the curse. So choose life, that you may live" (Deuteronomy 30:19). Make a good choice. The Maker of Heaven and Earth, Almighty God, Deliverer, Redeemer, Righteous King, Eternal Father is cheering you on!

A Prayer

Jesus, I am weary and tired. I feel like trash that has been put on the side of the road that even the trash collector will not pick up. I don't believe that I could ever be loved again or that I am worth loving. My heart aches from this wound of rejection. I ask you to give me strength to believe what is true, that I have value because you made me. Give me strength to believe my value is found in you.

This is such a lonely journey. The tears will not stop coming and I am growing weary of them. There are days when I'm not sure I can do this anymore. This place in life is too much for me to bear. This is not the way I dreamed it would be. This is not what I wanted.

Give me strength to see the value in my tears and to know that you will catch my tears. Hold me tight right now, for I am exhausted. Show me, Lord, that you are near. Put your hand on my head at night and take all of the thoughts that drive me into darkness. Give me strength to get up in the morning and be there for the precious gifts that you have given me. Encourage my heart that it may overflow into my children. And when the grief hits me once again like a tidal wave, give me the grace to embrace it and ride the wave knowing that this is part of the healing journey.

In Jesus' name, Amen.

God's Promises in Scripture

Jeremiah 29:11 *"For I know the plans that I have for you," declares the Lord, "plans for welfare and not for calamity to give you a future and a hope."*

Psalm 174:3 *"He heals the brokenhearted and binds up their wounds."*

Matthew 11:28–29 *"Come to Me, all who are weary and heavy-laden, and I will give you rest. Take My yoke upon you and learn from Me, for I am gentle and humble in heart, and you will find rest for your souls."*

Isaiah 40:29–31 *"He gives strength to the weary, and to him who lacks might He increases power. Though youths grow weary and tired, and vigorous young men stumble badly, yet those who wait for the Lord will gain new strength; They will mount up with wings like eagles, they will run and not get tired, they will walk and not become weary."*

Philippians 4:19 *"And my God will supply all your needs according to His riches in glory in Christ Jesus."*

Romans 8:37–39 *"But in all these things we overwhelmingly conquer through Him who loved us. For I am convinced that neither death, nor life, nor angels, nor principalities, nor things present, nor things to come, nor powers, nor height, nor depth, nor any other created thing, will be able to separate us from the love of God, which is in Christ Jesus our Lord."*

Proverbs 1:33 *"But he who listens to me shall live securely. And will be at ease from the dread of evil."*

John 14:27 *"Peace I leave with you; My peace I give to you; not as the world gives do I give to you. Do not let your heart be troubled, nor let it be fearful."*

Chapter 3

Steps to Freedom

By Sharon Kay Ball

The aftermath of divorce brings grief that often resembles bereavement of a death. Grief is the recognition that you have lost someone or something and cannot get them or it back. Divorce loss is devastating on many levels: emotional, spiritual, physical, and financial. It is the living death of your entire way of life. So, although you continue to live, your past and your future as you thought it would be ceases to exist.

As you walk through the stages of grief, it is important to know that grief is universal and it is different for each person. Generally people bounce around these stages. As you move through grief allow yourself to feel the movement, for where there is movement there is life, and where there is life there is hope. You will make it through, only to find yourself stronger. This is the gift of grief. It acknowledges how deep the loss is and then gives you strength to handle the depth of loss. Walk gently with yourself through these stages. Be kind, be still, and breathe. You will be amazed when you embrace your grief and no longer fear it. You will see it as your friend and not your enemy.

Shock and Denial

When you find yourself going through divorce, you will experience shock and denial. This occurs regardless of whether you wanted the divorce or not. Consider looking at it from the perspective of a tornado hitting your house. The damage is immense. There is nothing left of the house. At this point in time, reality may be too much for your heart to handle. It is natural to hold onto what you have known. Comfort is found in the known; however, your known is gone and you have to find a new normal.

Move into the reality that you are getting a divorce.

1. During this time it is important that you provide a consistent schedule for you and your children. Get a calendar, a rather large calendar. Put it in the kitchen and anytime an event comes up that you need to remember, write it down! In this season of your life it'll be hard to count on your memory. Don't worry, your memory will come back, but for now just write everything down.

2. Ask some friends to bring a meal to your house once or twice a week during the first couple of months of your divorce. Find some healthy frozen meals to pull out on days when you have no motivation to cook.

3. Ask for help when you need help. Life will feel like it is in the middle of a tornado and you will need help with everyday things for the first couple of months.

4. Choose close friends to put around your "roundtable." Your round table represents those people who you go to for advice. Limit this number to 3 or 4, because if you get too many people around your roundtable it can become very confusing. These people must have generous care and understanding for your situation. These people can provide insight and wisdom; however, honor the fact that this is your life and you make the final decisions.

Anger

There may be several sources of your anger during this part of your journey. However, I think at the heart of all these sources is the betrayal of your future, the way you hoped it would be. The dreams you and your partner shared for each other or for your children. It is these dreams that have died. These dreams existed even in a bad marriage where there is abuse and betrayal. Sometimes it is these dreams that keep women in those bad marriages. So when those dreams die, it exposes what really wasn't there. There is plenty to be angry about.

How you handle your anger during this time is key. What you do with your anger and how you act with it will determine whether it will be helpful to your recovery. Hurting someone with your anger will only make you feel good temporarily, but it will just put you in the same category as the person who hurt you. And remember, if you have children they are watching how you process this anger—you are their model.

🔊 Journal about your anger, allowing your thoughts to form on paper. In doing this you might find that the root of your anger is sadness, which may redirect your anger toward mourning your loss. Remind yourself that these thoughts are only thoughts; they do not have power unless put into action. It is when you act upon your anger that you can hurt others. Sometimes just seeing your thoughts written down diffuses what power they might have had. Should you become overwhelmed process these journal entries with your counselor.

⊱ Make a CD or playlist of your favorite, inspirational songs and listen to them when you feel the anger arise.

⊱ Exercise. Take some of the energy that anger brings and run it off!

⊱ Acknowledge your anger, don't stuff it. This anger is looking out for you. Anger is like an alert system, a warning sign that something is wrong. When anger is denied, it will sit within you and will surface in ways that you may not like. There is no way to get around anger.

Allow yourself to move through it, trusting that God put that emotion in you to alert you to the "wrongs" in life.

Sadness and Bargaining

Healing from divorce is long and hard. Sadness is often intertwined with anger. You may find yourself walking down memory lane going through all the "what if's," making a list of all the things you could have done to ensure a different outcome than divorce. Or you may feel amazing one day, only to run into someone at the grocery store who says something to you and it triggers a memory and then you are a weeping mess. This is normal. This is the dance grief does with you. Soon you will learn how to keep dancing with grief, even when you stumble the dance goes on.

During this process you are also discovering what it is like to live alone, to think alone, and dream alone. This can be terrifying and sad because this is not how you pictured your life to be. There are many adjustments being made in your life all at once. There are many decisions that need to be made and ironically all those decisions remind you of what has been lost.

Remember, you are grieving a death; it deserves your sadness. Grief reminds you of how much you loved what was lost. Expect sadness. It is good to be sad. Don't shy away from it. Tend to it wisely and you will move through it.

1. Be very kind and gentle to yourself. Use your journal to express your feelings.

2. Be open to seeking medical help if your feelings of sadness have altered your life in ways that affect your sleep, appetite, feelings of worthlessness, lack of motivation or pleasure in everyday life, or thoughts of suicide. Should you have these symptoms everyday for several weeks, please contact your physician or counselor.

3. Get out of the house. Do not isolate yourself. Go to the store, go to a park, volunteer at your child's school. Just get out and do something. This will allow you to see that life still exists!

Acceptance and Hope

Recovering from divorce is a slow process. It can—and often does—take several years to feel whole again. Use this time to love yourself again. When you can love yourself without judgment, then you can love others without judgment. Your capacity to love others mirrors your capacity to love yourself. Take your time with this. If you have taken your time with your grief, you will embrace your singleness. You may not always like being single, but you will be comfortable in your own single-skin.

During the first two years it is important that you focus on your grieving process and finding yourself as a single person again. This is not the time to become involved in a committed relationship. Your focus needs to be on rebuilding your self-esteem, your children's security, your friendships, and embracing your singleness. Most people exit their marriages with a wounded heart and until your heart has had time to heal, it will take that woundedness right into the next relationship. You will have given yourself the gift of grief and recovery, which will then be a gift to your future partner. There is hope for your future.

1. Give yourself time to explore your five senses. This will be a time for rediscovery. What kind of candle scents do you like? What kind of clothing material do you like to wear, but that you never noticed? Do you like to listen to music while you cook?

2. Give yourself enough time before you get into a serious relationship. Have fun dating. Discover what you like and don't like.

3. Celebrate your recovery process. Gather a few friends and reminisce about how far you have come. It may surprise you some of the memories they have about your strength that you have forgotten.

For Mothers Going through Divorce

It is important for you to recognize that you are a model for your children's grief. Your children are watching you. They need to see that even though you grieve, you will make it through life's challenges.

Allow them to grieve too. For children, their grief will mirror their developmental stage. Be active in understanding this for your children's sake. At the same time, grant yourself immeasurable amounts of grace because there will be days when all you can provide for them is a hot meal and a mother's hug. This is just as valuable as sitting down with them and verbally processing their loss.

Encourage the relationship with the other parent. The only time when this would not be good is in situations of abuse; seek a counselor's advice or legal advice.

Speak positively about the other parent. Your children are a part of your ex-spouse and when you put down the other parent, you not only hinder the relationship between your children and the parent, but your children will feel you are putting them down too.

Try to co-parent as much as possible for your children's sake. Attend your state's co-parenting class or seek professional counseling regarding how to do this.

Remember, your children have had the most changes due to this divorce. You and your ex's decisions need to be made for the best interest of your children and not yourself.

When in doubt on how to handle a situation, research and ask around. Education and knowledge are power!

OTHER BOOKS FROM THE FREEDOM SERIES

When divorce devastates a home, or a woman experiences abuse, paralyzing fear, abandonment, rape, or abortion, she needs God's restoration and wholeness. Michelle Borquez's **FREEDOM series** brings you true stories that show how to heal and experience joy again.

ABUSE TO FAVOR
When abuse happens, as women we tend to take on the pain alone. But you aren't alone and you don't have to deal with it alone. This book helps women understand that it's not your fault and you don't have to face it alone. Paperback, 4.5"x 6.5", 96 pages.

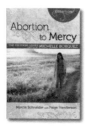

ABORTION TO MERCY
You never thought you would be in the situation of having an abortion and once it's over the pain is still there. But God has not left you because of this one action. This book helps you heal and move past the hurt. Paperback, 4.5"x 6.5", 96 pages.

DIVORCE TO WHOLENESS
Divorce can tear you in half. It's not easy to deal with or sometimes even understand. With *Divorce to Wholeness* you learn how to put yourself back together and become whole again. Paperback, 4.5"x 6.5", 96 pages.

FEAR TO COURAGE

Fear to Courage shows women that they don't have to be a slave to their fears and helps them truly define their fears and develop the courage to move past them. This book shows women that through Christ all things are possible. Paperback, 4.5"x 6.5", 96 pages.

ABANDONMENT TO FORGIVENESS

At some point in every woman's life she has felt a sense of abandonment, for some this feeling is bigger than others. This book teaches women that no matter who has left you, God is always with you. Paperback, 4.5"x 6.5", 96 pages.

DECEIVED TO DELIVERED

She never thought she would cross the line and have an affair, but she did. *Deceived to Delivered* shows women how to strengthen their boundaries and restore their relationships. Paperback, 4.5"x 6.5", 96 pages.